BANZAI

BOOK OF BETTING

First published 2002 by Channel 4 Books
an imprint of Pan Macmillan Ltd
Pan Macmillan, 20 New Wharf Road, London N1 9RR
Basingstoke and Oxford
Associated companies throughout the world
www.panmacmillan.com

0 7522 6209 2

1 3 5 7 9 8 6 4 2

A CIP catalogue record for this book
is available from the British Library.

Designed by seagulls
Printed by Butler and Tanner, Frome and London

This book accompanies the television series Banzai,
produced by Radar Productions Ltd. for Channel 4.

WARNING
Remember, these bets should only be attempted in the presence of a
well-trained and experienced gambler man. Do not attempt these bets at
home alone. We cannot accept liability for any loss or damage to any
person acting as a result of the information contained in this book.
You have been warned.

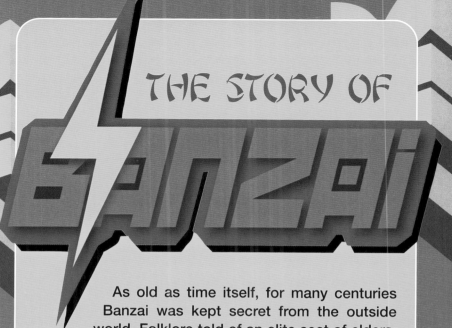

THE STORY OF BANZAI

As old as time itself, for many centuries Banzai was kept secret from the outside world. Folklore told of an elite sect of elders, high in the mountains, who practised a gambling martial art so extreme that many thought it was simply a myth or a fantasy.

Death, disease and the weather were all things (legend has it) that they gambled upon.

For centuries the art of Banzai was practised in complete isolation. Beautifully crafted wagers were constructed, whose intricacy would often leave spectators dizzy with their genius – gambles within gambles; bets within bets… where would it all end?

Sadly, after many years of extreme betting, the elders realised they had gambled away everything they had once owned. Nothing was left, all was gone. So, strapped for cash they decided that there was only one option left open to them.

The chief of the elders slowly and painstakingly wrote down all their ancient gambles in a book crafted from the wood of the final tree left in their once great forest. Written in the blood of an owl, it was truly a thing of exquisite beauty. He even drew a big 'B' on the cover.

Then, one cold and chilly November morn two of the youngest elders bade farewell to their loved ones and travelled down from the mountaintop to the city. The hopes and dreams of the entire Banzai tribe now lay with them.

For many days they wandered in the wilderness, cold and hungry. Inevitably, they began to place cunning wagers with each other to wile away the hours of the journey. Sadly they had nothing to bet with so they resorted to gambling away parts of their own bodies.

Finally, after many days, they saw in the distance, with their one good eye, the bright lights of the city. As quickly as they could, they hopped into town and began to seek the fortune that would save their friends and families back home on the mountain.

When they saw the many wonders of the city it filled their hearts with excitement and wonder. Stuff like umbrellas, the music of Mr Brian May from Queen, tins of meat and moustaches. So many new gambling opportunities, yet so little time.

Within days of their arrival they had set up a house of Banzai in a shady part of the city. Slowly the crowds began to grow, bewitched by these strangers' gambling devilry. The beauty of their bets seduced even the coldest of hearts and soon they had won enough money to buy new clothes, food, drink, women and prosthetic limbs.

The house of Banzai grew larger and larger. Times were good. There seemed to be an everlasting supply of gambles to call upon from the ancient book. Then one day a man from a large television company entered the house of Banzai. He showed them pictures of Chris Evans with Billie, Westlife and A1, and the sitcom 'Three up, two down' with Boon in it. Truly, anything was possible in this man's world.

That night they drank too much rice wine and drunkenly showed the television man the ancient book of Banzai bets. Immediately he asked them how much they would sell it to him for. The two Banzai elders laughed out loud. Ha. Did this man understand nothing? Could he be so blind?

Banzai was not for sale. Banzai is for everyone. It is a way of life... it is the air that you breathe, the wind beneath your wings. It caresses your soul when you sleep and gives meaning to your every waking hour. It is in the space between love and hate, peace and war, Hale and Pace. They couldn't sell Banzai, because it was not theirs to sell.

The television man wiped the tears from his eyes and said it was a pity because he was going to give them enough money to put a deposit down on a reasonable sized semi in Surrey.

Later that week, the entire Banzai tribe moved to the leafy suburbs of Godalming, a charming town that is situated in some of the finest countryside in southern England. Apparently the man who lives next door but one used to sing with Mike And The Mechanics. Banzai had arrived.

THOUGHT FOR THE DAY

Monday

If joke isn't funny, repeat while laughing.

Snort occasionally for added effect.

The Little Furry Friend Flutter

If you are a lonely person, then probably your only friend will be a pet. So play Banzai with your little furry friend and a phone. Every time you get a gamble wrong you must dial one number of your local vet. If you get enough bets wrong, the number will be dialled in full. You must then speak to the animal doctor and ask them to put your little furry friend to sleep... FOREVER. So sad.

Why not invite the couple next door round to play Banzai. Normally you will find that more than one person will get a gamble correct. When this is the case, the winners must do it proper with each other immediately. If just one person gets it right, they must do it proper with themselves while everyone watches. It's soooo much fun.

The Naughty Naughty Bet Bit

The Old Lady Confectionery Conundrum

If you are an old lady, then all you need to play Banzai is another old lady and one boiled sweet. Every time an old lady gets a gamble correct, they get to suck on the delicious everlasting sweet. Whichever old lady is left in control of the sweet at the end of the game is the winner. The losing old lady must then dance the Riverdance dance for everyone's enjoyment until the sun in the sky says goodbye.

Why not play Banzai with a bunch of Jewish friends and a wooden cross? Every time you get a gamble wrong one of your friends will hammer a part of your body to the cross. If, during the game, you unfortunately pass away then you are a loser. However, if you come back from the dead then you are a winner and possibly the Son of God… or a ghost.

A Blessed Big Bet Proposal

The Man of Pain Tennis Torment

If you are a gimp man, then why not play Banzai with another gimp man and the international tennis player Mr Andre Agassi man. Every time a gimpman gets a gamble right, Mr Agassi man will serve a high-speed ball at gimpman's private region as a reward. The gimpman who collects the most private points at the end of the game is the winner. If you cannot get Mr Agassi man do not worry. A Tim Henman man will do.

THOUGHT FOR THE DAY

Tuesday

There is no such thing as a bad loser. No one will ever want to do it proper with you again, is all.

WHO IS WHO PLEASE?

A mystery figure that is like an enigma wrapped within a conundrum. His call to gamble, sung in a voice so soft and sweet, always begins and ends each Banzai betting session. He also makes sure fair play is carried out at all times during any Banzai tournament. His favourite film is *Silver Dream Machine* starring David Essex.

Mr Banzai

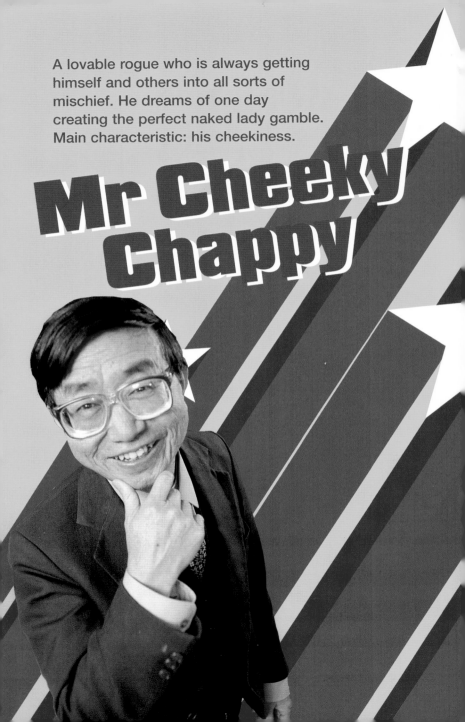

A lovable rogue who is always getting himself and others into all sorts of mischief. He dreams of one day creating the perfect naked lady gamble. Main characteristic: his cheekiness.

Mr Cheeky Chappy

The Animal Scientists

Men in white coats gamble with animals in a scientifically justifiable fashion. Their motto is 'progress leads to knowledge'. Knowledge leads to truth. The search for truth leads to... animal scientific experiments.

A stunningly beautiful temptress who likes to ask celebrity people only one question. Celebrity people taunt and challenge her for more but she always resists and maintains a wall of silence against them. Question is how long will it be before the celebrity people get bored and walk away? Personal best: 157 seconds of silence against Mr Bob Holness man.

Lady One Question

Mr Shake Hands Man

Mr Shake Hands Man like to shake hands with celebrity people for long time. Question is how long you think he shake hands with celebrity people for, eh? His personal best was four minutes and thirty-two seconds with Miss Donna Air lady.

The Backwards Chinese Detective

The Backwards Chinese Detective is only detective with power to reverse the laws of time. Mr and Mrs Badman watch out because crime costs and right here is where you start paying.

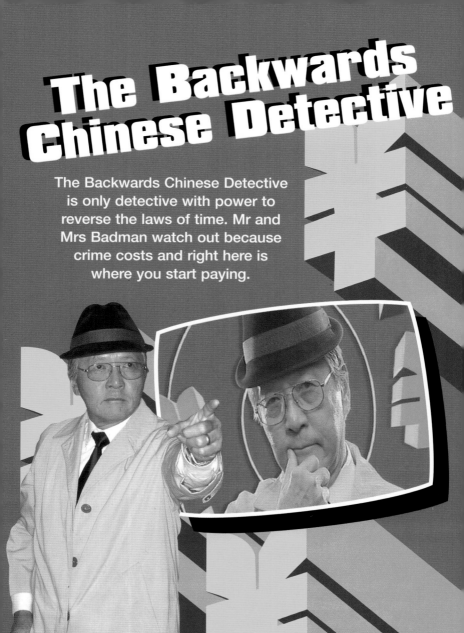

Mr Shake Hands Man liked to shake hands with celebrity people for long time but sadly, celebrity people got to know his face and no one want to shake his hand anymore.

The solution was simple. Replace him with... Mr Shake Hands Man 2. He do exactly the same thing as Mr Shake Hands Man 1... only he a lot fatter. His personal best was two minutes and forty-three seconds with Miss Thora Birch lady from Hollywood.

Mr Shake Hands Man 2

Many thought she was gone, but she has returned as Diana – the paranormal plastic doll of justice. She answers questions from beyond the grave with the help of her psychic parachute of truth. Simply ask the doll a question then throw it out of the window of a tall building. Marked on the ground are the words 'Yes' and 'No'. Wherever she lands – that is the answer to your question.

Princess Diana

Wednesday

What's the point in breathing if you're not betting?

Ask Mr Shake Hands Man

How did you learn to be such a great shake hands man?

I was taught the ancient way of the shake by a crack team of Banzai monks. They found me as a small boy and raised me as their own. I was only four when I first began to shake properly, but even then I realised I had a special gift. As time passed, my shakings drew great crowds from all the local villages. After a two-day shake with Jamahl Van Batson (he is similar in stature to Mr Chris Rea), I realised that it was time to share my gift with the rest of the world.

What do you think of when you are in a shake?

I tend to go into a Zen-like state when I am shaking. Everything else seems to melt away. All that matters to me is the connection I feel between the celebrity and myself. Sometimes I can get distracted by little things, for example, I found Mr Keith Duffy to have very soft and small hands, which I like. But I tend not to dwell on these things; you must always compose yourself quickly and get on with the job.

What are the five grips of shakeyness?

Technically there are five grips of shakeyness you need to perfect before you can truly call yourself a shake hands man.

Grip one – 'The lady'

Wrap your hand gently around the fingers of your guest and begin a soft shaking motion up and down. Celebrities who enjoy this are most boy band members, children's TV presenters and Mr Prince Edward royal man.

Grip two – 'The turtle'

Place your first finger over the side knuckle of your guest and hold their fingers with your remaining three fingers. See thumb section for thumb options. Celebrities who enjoy this include Mr Sting, Mrs Dido and Mr Keanu.

Grip three – 'The rabbits ears'

Place your first two fingers over the side knuckle of your guest and hold their fingers with your remaining two fingers. Celebrities who enjoy this include Mr Melvyn Bragg, the cast of *Brush Strokes* and Professor Stephen Hawkins (he has a plastic hand moulded in the shape of this grip that he produces from out of his chair when meeting other scientists).

Grip four – 'The trident'

Place your first three fingers over the side knuckle of your guest and hold their fingers with your remaining one finger. Celebrities who enjoy this include Catherine Zeta Jones, Dannii Minogue and Charlotte Church (now she is past the age of consent).

Grip five – 'The devil's claw'

A particularly difficult grip. Place all four of your fingers over the side knuckle of your guest and shake fiercely. Only one celebrity likes it like this... Mr Steve Davis from the world of snooker.

THE THUMB

The thumb can be placed into two positions whilst shaking:

A) 'The tuck'

Slip your thumb in the space between the thumb and first finger. This should not be done sexily, but firmly and smoothly. If you feel you have a compatible shaking partner then this is the recommended option.

B) 'The lock'

A very controversial thumb position especially when combined with 'the devil's claw'. The thumb is placed over your guest's thumb, restricting any possible thumb movement. This should only be used in extremely difficult shaking circumstances, such as when your guest is reluctant to even shake your hand once. If this is the case then they probably deserve everything they get.

Have you ever refused to shake someone's hand?

Everybody has his dark days. Personally, I prefer not to discuss them too much since the sun always rises again. One time though, I refused to shake hands with Mr Kenny G. I saw him come out of the gentlemen's toilets without washing. It tears me apart to think that a man of such greatness could have such little regard for the art of shaking.

What are your hopes for the future?

My dream is to one day shake the hand of Mr Phil Collins for at least twenty-four hours non-stop. He is a genius and I am a big fan of his work, in particular his 'Sussudio' period. To think that this might happen fills me with joy.

I would also like to bring my shaking to the West End. I'm a big fan of the musical *Starlight Express* and would be interested in any similar offers to put on this style of production with Sir Andrew Lloyd Webber and Sir Richard Stilgoe.

Thursday

Give a man a fish and he will eat for a day.

Give a man a fishing rod and he will sell it and get a takeaway.

PLAY AT HOME FUN

Banzai is proud to present a super selection of gambling opportunities for you to try out for yourself.

1. The Old Lady Wheelchair Chicken Challenge

Find two old ladies in electric wheelchairs. Park one old lady exactly 50 metres away from other old lady and point them towards each other. On the signal, each old lady must drive her wheelchair in a straight line towards the other old lady. Collision course is inevitable unless one old lady pulls away. Which old lady will chicken out first?

HAZEL

DOT

Will it be Hazel or Dot?

PLACE YOUR BETS

BETTING ENDS

Look, old lady Hazel, she chicken out. Not by much, but she chicken, so she lose. Congratulations to Dot and everyone who knows her.

2. Supermarket Trolley Cake Jumping

Rules of supermarket trolley cake jumping very simple. A man or a lady must first sit in an everyday supermarket trolley. He or she is then pushed at great speed towards a ramp by a friend of the family. Beyond the ramp lie ten Sarah Lee Double Chocolate Gateaux Cakes. Object of game is to jump over as many cakes as possible. Remember: trolley must clear each cake completely, otherwise it doesn't count.

Cakes must be 15cm across and are spaced 8 cm apart. Trolley must be made of mild steel and weigh about 32 kg.

So, how many cakes you think they jump, eh?

Will it be:
A) 2
B) 4
C) 6
D) 8
E) 10

PLACE YOUR BETS

If you bet Mr Matt would clear eight cakes, then congratulations. He's shown that courage is a dish best served whole.

3. The Small Animal Balloon Lift Gamble

Take one chicken and bundles of floaty helium balloons. Now begin to slowly attach floaty balloons to the chicken. Question is, how many floaty balloons will it take to lift chicken straight up in air?

Will it be:
A) 30
B) 60
C) 90
Or D) 120?

PLACE YOUR BETS

BETTING ENDS

We have lift off. If you said 90 balloons, you spot on. Look at that flying chicken. Goodbye, Larry, we salute your ultimate sacrifice at the altar of science.

4. Squirrel Fishing

To begin squirrel fishing you will need a long fishing rod with long piece of string attached to it. At the end of the line you will need some bait to attract a squirrel. A nut will normally do. Now go to a squirrel park and hide in a bush or up a tree and cast out your nut. When squirrels takes your bait, wait until they have got a good grip on the nut and then try and lift the little furry fellow off the ground. Whoever can lift a squirrel the highest is the winner!

Today's brave squirrel competitors are the mighty Vangelis and the deadly Marzipan. Who will be lifted off the ground first?

VANGELIS

MARZIPAN

PLACE YOUR BETS

5. The Tramp Beer Temptation

Put a full beer can of super-strength lager down next to some dirty tramps. How long will it be before they pick it up and guzzle it? Will it be:

A) 0 to 20 seconds
B) 20 to 40 seconds
Or C) 40 to 60 seconds?

PLACE YOUR BETS

BETTING ENDS

Stop the clock! If you bet 40 seconds,
you are a winner!

6. Ye Olde Supermarket Trolley Jousting Tournament

To play this game you will need two knights. One dressed in white – he the good man. And one dressed in black – he the bad man. They both will carry a weapon of destruction that look a little like a mop.

Each must ride his supermarket trolley towards the other at great speed and attempt to push his opponent out of his trolley. If you fall, you lose, understand? Good.

So, who you think is champion Supermarket Trolley Joust man?

Whitey or Blacky?

Whitey or Blacky?

Whitey or Blacky?

PLACE YOUR BETS

BETTING ENDS

Congratulations Black Knight.
You are the king of Jousting Trolley Tournament.

7. The Genital Weight Gamble With Mr Peter Beale

This Mr Peter Beale. He famous for being the father of Ian Beale and for running the fruit and veg stall now owned by Mark Fowler in *EastEnders*. That was a long time ago and he's still not famous for much else!

Question is, how much do you think his meat and two veg weigh? Is it the same as:

A) Two satsumas and a baby courgette
B) Three ripe plums
Or C) A small bunch of bananas?

PLACE YOUR BETS

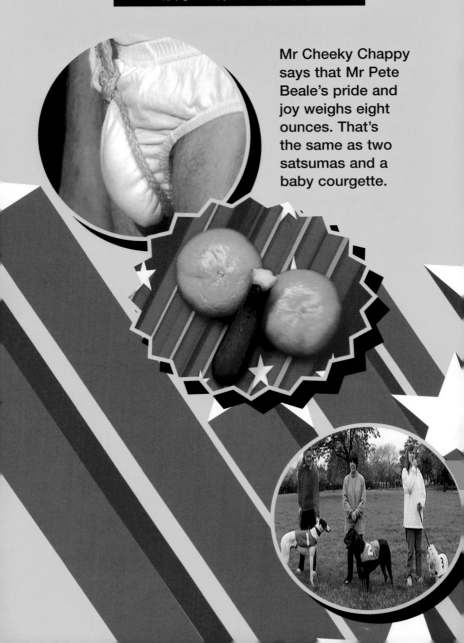

Mr Cheeky Chappy says that Mr Pete Beale's pride and joy weighs eight ounces. That's the same as two satsumas and a baby courgette.

8. The Dog Toilet Torment Challenge

Take three different doggies. Maybe a greyhound, a Rottweiler or a poodle or something, I don't know, I'm not a dog expert! Feed them lots of food then take them out to a big field with lots of trees. Question is, when you release the doggies in the field, which one will go to the toilet first? Place your bets now.

PLACE YOUR BETS

BETTING ENDS

It's the skinny greyhound Jimmy doing a jimmy.

9. The Blessed Bucket Of Bibles Bet

Here's a fun way of testing the strength of a rabbi who has a beard and a hat and everything. Rules of godlike gamble quite simple. Rabbi must take two metal buckets full of Jewish Bibles and hold them out in front of himself for as long as possible. Game ends as soon as metally style buckets hit metally style tabletop causing small red bulb to light up. Understand? Good.

So, how long do you think genuine rabbi manage to hold on to his buckets for? Will it be:
A) Less than 30 seconds
B) Between 31 to 40 seconds
Or C) 41 to 300 seconds?

PLACE YOUR BETS

He made 55 seconds.
If you bet on 'C', you are a winner!

10. The Andy Crane Spin Cycle Rodeo

Rules of domestic apparatus gamble quite simple. Get a Mr Andy Crane to place two objects on top of a washing machine. For example, two tiny boy members of pop group, Steps, and the mighty Scrabble, the once sleeping, now dead cat. Ha-ha. Then get him to set the machine on super-speed spin cycling. Object which stays on top of jumping washing machine the longest is the winner. Understand? Good.

PLACE YOUR BETS

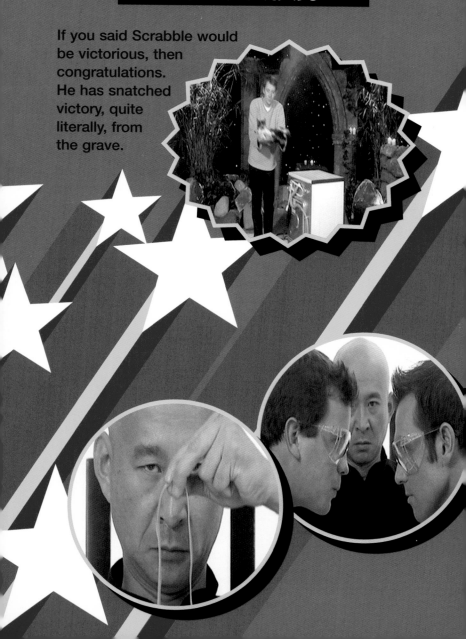

BETTING ENDS

If you said Scrabble would be victorious, then congratulations. He has snatched victory, quite literally, from the grave.

11. The Fantastic Elastic Band Bet

Take two stupid people and one big fantastic elastic band. First place a pair of funny looking glasses on each stupid person. Next, get them to take hold of the fantastic elastic band in their teeth. On a command, they must then pull back to one of the numbered sections on the table. If the band breaks or if one of them lets go then the winner is the one left holding the fantastic elastic in their teeth.

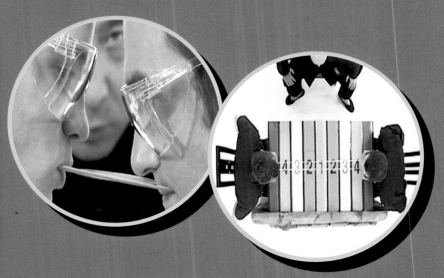

Will it be Mr Peter or Mr Nick?

PLACE YOUR BETS

BETTING ENDS

If you back Mr Nick man, you are a winner.
He got a face full of rubber.

12. The Fantastic Freddie Man Flutter

Rules of Mercury man gamble very simple. Take three men dressed as Mr Freddie Mercury man from Queen. Each Freddie must then hang onto a traditional football crossbar for as long as possible using only their hands. If a Freddie man falls, he lose. Last Freddie hanging is the winner.

Who will it be:
A: Bohemian Freddie
B: Live Aid Freddie
C: Leather Freddie?

PLACE YOUR BETS

BETTING ENDS

Ready Freddies?

WINNER
WINNER
WINNER

Bohemian Freddie,
you are a champion.
What a tribute to the
great man you are!

13. The Roundabout Of Righteousness roulette

Find a group of men dressed as Mr Adolph Hitler man. Then find another group of men dressed as Mr Ghandi man. Now place them all on an everyday roundabout.

You must now stand in front of roundabout and spin it right round, baby right round, like a record baby. Question is, who will you be facing when the big wheel stops spinning? Will it be Mr Ghandi man or Mr Hitler man?

PLACE YOUR BETS

BETTING ENDS

If you picked Hitler,
then you're a
winner!

14. The Little Chocolate Ball Blow Bet

Take two pretty model ladies, a little chocolate ball and a big, long plastic tube. Rules of confectionery challenge simple. The little ball of chocolate is placed in the middle of the plastic tube. Each lady must then blow super hard into tube and attempt to make sweet travel into opponent's mouth. Winner is the lady who makes her opponent chomp on the little ball first. Understand? Good.

PLACE YOUR BETS

BETTING ENDS

It's all gone. It's in Jodie's mouth – she is a loser! Congratulations, Lisa B. Your blowing's second to none.

15. The Dog Poo Stinky Show Showdown

Take two men of business who both think this town isn't big enough for the both of them. In front of them you place six handsome businessmen shoes that look oh so smart mister. However, although they all look very comfortable and shiny, one shoe hides a dark brown secret. Mr Cheeky Chappy has filled one of them with genuine dog droppings. Why? Because he so cheeky!

Businessmen must take it in turns to select one shoe for their foot. Game ends when one man becomes a brown-toed loser and picks the stinky poo shoe.

Who gets the poo? Jean-Paul or Fred?

PLACE YOUR BETS

BETTING ENDS

Oh no, Mr Fred has found the poo shoe. He not look happy!

16. Men Of Brick War Of China

Take two builder men who have big shiny helmets. Give them three commemorative tea mugs of royalty. Now ask them kindly to walk ten paces away from each other and then turn around. On the command they must now take it in turns to throw a mug at each other. If they smash a mug on their opponent's helmet, then that is a hit. If they hit their body or face, it simply not count at all. The one with the most hits at the end of the game is a winner.

Will it be Black Knight or White Knight?

PLACE YOUR BETS

BETTING ENDS

Glorious throwings
from the White Knight.
If you bet on him you
back a real winner.

17. The Family Fun Specimen Showdown

Liven up any family party with this fun game. Ask three family men, like your dad, grandad and funny uncleman, to play. Give each of them one naughty naughty lady magazine to read. On the command they must all go behind surgical screens provided to read the magazine. The first to deposit the sticky gift of life into special Banzai beaker is the winner.

Who will it be?
Place your
bets now!

PLACE YOUR BETS

If you say number 1 you are a winner!

18. A Sticky Stamp Invitation Situation

Nominate one person to play the anarchist. Now get anarchist person to stick out their tongue once and once only. Question is, using only the sticking power of one tongues worth of anarchist spit, how many stamps, with Queen's head on it, can be moistened and made to glue to a stack of letters you need posting? Come on bet now! What you think? How many stamps they stick?

A) 1–5 stamps
B) 6–10 stamps
Or C) 11–15 stamps?

PLACE YOUR BETS

BETTING ENDS

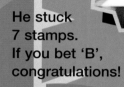

He stuck
7 stamps.
If you bet 'B',
congratulations!

19. A Very Interesting Beefeater Investigation Question

Collect two beefmen from the Tower of London. Now give each beefman identical trays that both contain five different and delicious cold meats. For example: turkey roll, roast ham, salami, corned beef and ox tongue.

Sit both beefmen at opposite ends of a table and place a dividing screen between them. Now lower the screen so they cannot see each other. On the command, ask each beefman to pick up and hold out one piece of meat in front of them. Using only their psychic beefman magic that helps to guard the Queen, they must now try and make the same meat selection as each other. If they both pick the same, then one meat point is scored. If they make a different selection then it don't count at all. It so easy.

So question is, out of three selections, how many times will the beefmen's psychic powers work? How much meat will they match?

Remember, it like a game of cold meat snap.

Will they match:
A) No meats at all
B) Only 1 meat
C) 2 meats
Or D) all 3 meats?

PLACE YOUR BETS

BETTING ENDS

Those beefmen
very clever.
They matched
all three
meats!

20. The Tug Tug Tissue Test

Any number of people can play this game, but for the purposes of this instruction we will describe a two-player game. Position each player in front of a normal everyday household toilet paper dispenser. Inside is one roll of new toilet paper that is rolled around its cardboardy tube. On word 'go', each player has to begin unrolling their roll as quick as possible. First player to reach the cardboard tube is the winner.

This not as easy as it sounds, experience shows hasty players can easily pull too fast and hard, leading to snappings of their toilet paper, which cause costly delays as the end is found again.

Will it be:
A) Davro
B) Kamara?

PLACE YOUR BETS

BETTING ENDS

If you bet on Kamara, then you are a winner!

THOUGHT FOR THE DAY

Friday

A wink off a friend is not always a good omen.

He may have something in his eye.

A QUICK ONE WITH MR CHEEKY CHAPPY

Mr Cheeky Chappy has selected a number of super speedy gambles for you to play at home either by yourself or with someone you love. Have big fun.

1. The Celebrity Sexy Party Selection

Mr John McCririck is an eccentric TV horseman. Tonight, he is holding a sexy party with a fellow minor celebrity acquaintance – Mr Chris Quentin who used to be in Coronation Street, a long time ago.

To help sexy party go with a swing, Mr John and Mr Chris get to pick two lovely ladies each from our Banzai bed. But that means one nice lady will be left on shelf. Which one will it be?

Do you think it will be:
A) Miss Celeste
B) Miss Nancy
C) Miss Rachel
D) Miss Angela
Or E) Miss Jackie?

PLACE YOUR BETS

BETTING ENDS

Unbelievable... it's blondie lady called Nancy. If you said she'd be the one not invited to the minor celebrity sexy party, you are a winner!

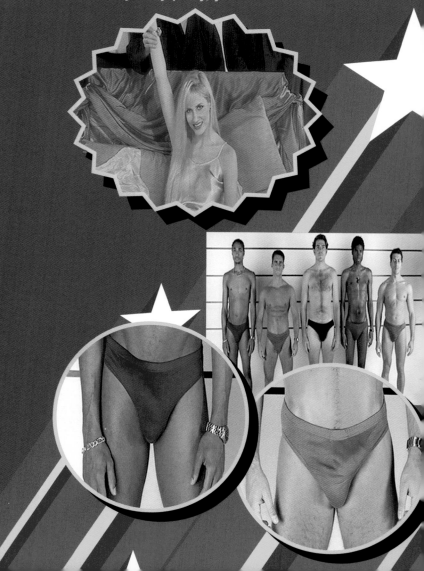

2. The Generous Portioned Gentleman Gamble

Five gentlemen, one has been blessed with a genuine super-large lady pleaser; the other four are not so lucky. Their aim is to deceive by stuffing socks down their underpants. So, can you tell whose monster size package is the real thing? Number one perhaps? Impressive. What about number two? Ah, very nice! Maybe it number three? No, probably not. Could it be number four? Ooh, marvellous! Or, perhaps it number five. What a smashing bloke! Okay, so which one is the genuine generous portion gentleman?

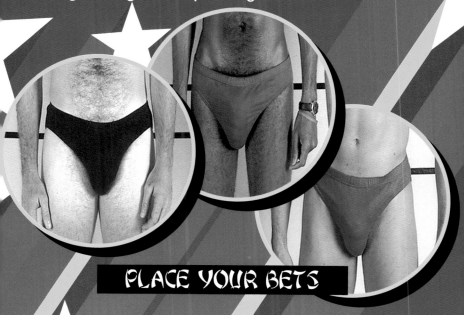

PLACE YOUR BETS

3. The Trouserless Cricket Man Conundrum

This Mr Philip Tufnell. He top English cricketer who represent his country many times against great oppositions round the world. But that's not important. Question is, which one of these bottoms belongs to Mr Tufnell?

Is it number one… peachy? Or number two… cheeky? Could it be number three… spotty? Or number four… blimey! Or maybe number five… shiny? Which one you think?

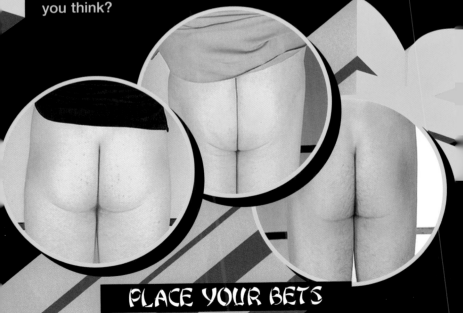

PLACE YOUR BETS

BETTING ENDS

If you said number two – you are a winner!

4. The Lying Lady Puzzle

Five nice pretty ladies who any man would be proud to maybe have a kiss and a cuddle with. But beware, for appearances can be deceptive. One of them ain't no lady; she's a bloke. Can you tell which one is the she man? Is it number one. Is her toilet seat up or down? Or number 2? What lies behind that mysterious smile? Could it be number 3? Is she a he or is she a she... maybe she both. What about number 4? Mmm, very difficult decision, isn't it? Or is it number 5? She got earrings bigger than her ears! Maybe that's important. I don't know! The question is which lady is actually a bloke?

PLACE YOUR BETS

BETTING ENDS

If you said number four, congratulations – you sorting the man out from the boys 'cos she the he.

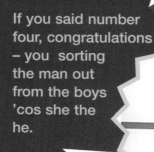

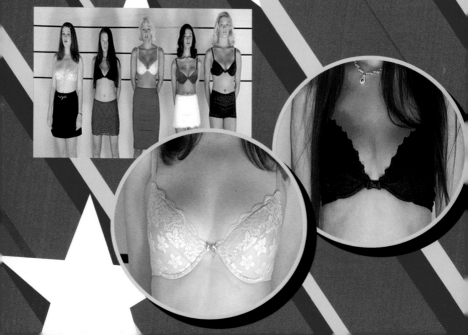

5. The Lying Breast Puzzle

Five nice ladies, four as nature intended. One, however, has had a big breast operation. Can you tell which one?

Could it be nice lady number one? Lovely! What about number two? Very nice. Number three? Good, good. Number four? Ooh my! Or number five – blimey, many thanks.

Which one has had the operation?

PLACE YOUR BETS

BETTING ENDS

If you said number three, you have got it right 'cos she the lady who's had them done.
Outstanding!

6. The Wig Man Line Up

Five gentlemen, four of them have full head of hair, one is a baldy bloke who hides his shame beneath a wig. Can you tell which one he is? Is he number one? I hope for his sake it is! Or perhaps it is number two. He not very happy about something. Number three? Has he got a touch of Wogan about him? Number four? He look a bit dodgy don't you think? Or number five? Who look like a cross between Bobby Charlton and Mr Adolf Hitler?

So, which one you think the genuine baldy bloke?

PLACE YOUR BETS

If you said number four, congratulations,
may prosperity shine upon your household
during the winter months.

7. The Bachelor Bra Buy Set

This is John. He a genuinely confirmed bachelor boy who has an eye for ladies fashion, particularly ladies underwear.

Question is, which type of ladies under things you think ring his bachelor bell?

Will it be underwear style number one – it some sort of black lacy number, very nice.

Maybe it number two – a very classy cream silky thing. Lovely.

Final outfit is number three – a big red sexy nightie. Oh my, she very saucy lady indeed.

Okay, which one do you think his favourite?
A) Black and lacy
B) Creamy silky
C) Red naughty?

PLACE YOUR BETS

BETTING ENDS

Oh, it's the creamy silky thing – what splendid bachelor bra buy pickings.

8. The Famous Man Dingle Dangle Dilemma

A long time ago, there was a man called Mr Normski. He was famous for saying things like 'wicked' and 'enough respect' on BBC2 television. But that not important. Question is, can you tell which one is his dingle dangle? Could it be number one? Some people say that dogs look just like their owners. Is the same true of floppy man bit? Or is it number two? Blimey, you don't get many of them to the pound Mister. Look at number 3. Blimey. Don't feed the animals. Ha ha! Number four now. Is he going bald? Does he need a wig or something? Finally could it be number five? I'm no doctor but that no right. So, which lady pleaser you think belong to our celebrity friend Mr Normski?

PLACE YOUR BETS

BETTING ENDS

If you choose number two…
congratulations, they his privates
on parade. Thank you, Mr Normski
man, you are so professional.

9. The Dirty Old Grandma Gamble

Five lovely old ladies. Four of them have not been intimate with a gentleman for some time. One old lady, however, still go like the clappers. She a horny old pensioner who like to be pictured doing it proper in dirty magazines. Question is, can you spot the top shelf senior citizen? Is it lady number one? Does she know how to suck more than eggs, eh? Could it be number two? Does she go to bed with more than cup of cocoa? Nudge, nudge, wink, wink. What about old lady number three? She may have a face like a sore bottom but would you pay good money to watch her do it proper? Is it number four? She may not have her own teeth but maybe that a bonus in her line of work. Finally number five? Would you like to do it Granny style with her? So which one is the genuine dirty filthy old lady?

PLACE YOUR BETS

BETTING ENDS

Oh no ho ho. What she doing?
Call the police. If you picked
pensioner number four...
you are a winner!

10. The Lying Little Lady Puzzle

Five pretty young girls all in a row. All hoping to be crowned queen at this year's Banzai beauty pageant. Unfortunately, one of these lovely young lady beauty queens is an impostor. She is a little fella.

Question is, can you sort the boy out from the girls? Could it be number one? Is this little blondie lady a trainee transvestite? What about number two? Could she be the junior gender bender? Here's number three. Is she really a little lady boy? Number four. Could it be that she one of them? Finally number five. Is this little lady a little laddie? Eh? What you think?

Which young lady is not what she seems? Who is the little man, eh?

PLACE YOUR BETS

BETTING ENDS

If you said number three... you the man!
He's the real tiny transvestite. Well done, my son.
Don't worry, it's just a phase you're going through.

THOUGHT FOR THE DAY

Saturday

The man who does not learn is like one walking in the night. Soon he will get the urge to eat a kebab.

How to make your own wheel of misfortune

Mr Banzai believes you can increase play-at-home fun by making your own wheel of misfortune as follows…

First, find an old flask that you no longer use. Or borrow one from a friend or a neighbour and simply never give it back.

Now remove the plastic cup add on, please. Thank you.

Carefully mix some cement and place it on the bottom area of the flask. Quickly fix this to a central position on your dining table. When it is dry then that is your spinning column complete.

Now you need to make a spinning plate that has a hole in the centre big enough to slot over the flask. The whole plate should be 24 inches in diameter and have some wheels on the bottom that will allow it to spin around smoothly.

Once that is done, split the plate up into six equal segments. You can then paint the segments different colours if you like or simply decorate them with meat or cheese.

Now slip the plate over the column and spin it around.

OK. It's time for action. Load up each segment of the wheel with six potentially dangerous items. Now disarm five of them but leave one still active.

Ideas for wheel ammo

Brolley

Place six spring activated umbrellas on the wheel. Five of the brollies have had their springs deactivated, so only one will now spring open at the touch of a button. Two players must use great courage and take it in turns at shooting the brollies into their faces. If they pick up broke one, they okay – if not, they lose not only the game but maybe a few teeth as well.

Egg

Place six eggs on the wheel of misfortune. Five of them are hard-boiled, but one of them still retains its full runny yolky magnificence. Two players must take it in turns to pick up egg and smash it in their faces. They must continue until one is left with runny egg all over his face. He's the loser.

Mystery fizz can

Place six cans of beer on the wheel. Five cans nice to drink, one can not nice, someone has shaken it all up and will now explode in your face. Each player must be brave and pick a can then open it in front of his face.

Hair mousse

On the wheel are six cans of hair mousse. Five of them have faulty nozzles and dispense nothing but thin air. One can, however, is still able to dispense large amounts of foaming white hair product. Each player must take it in turns to choose a can then poke it up his nose and then... fire. Whoever suffers moussey misery is the loser.

Sunday

If you wear Brut aftershave you will attract a cheap woman

Wisdom from the Banzai Master

And now, with the end near, it is time to face a final curtain. Remember, as Mr Peter Gabriel said, it is better to have loved and left Genesis, than to stay and let Collins man write 'Invisible Touch'.

He who laughs last laughs loudest, unless you have a voice box and then it depends on the volume.

A woman's work is never done, unless she's unemployed and really lazy.

Crime doesn't pay, but *Crimewatch* does – Mr Nick Ross man, he so rich.

Always remember, in the true spirit of Banzai, when it is dark, turn the light on.

They say shake the bottle, wake the drink, but shake the hand and enjoy a life of eternal happiness.

Don't cut off your nose to spite your face, unless you are Gerard Depardieu and then you may be doing it a favour.

Give credit where credit's due, not to Cheeky Chappy, he such a poor gambler.

If ever confronted with angry famous man or famous lady in supermarket, shout down their ear with unbounded joy and enthusiasm – BANZAI!

Remember, the things that come to those who wait may be the things left by those who got there first!

When Lao-Tzu was asked, 'what is the way?' he replied, 'the way that can be spoken of is not the constant way. The name that can be named is not the constant name'. Sounds to me like he just didn't know.

Wise man say a gambling man is a foolish man. This man give you 3/1 on that he wrong.